FAMOUS FAMILIES

THE WACHOWSKI BROTHERS
CREATORS OF THE MATRIX

CHRISTY MARX

The Rosen Publishing Group, Inc., New York

In memory of Katherine. I wish she could have taken the blue pill.

Published in 2005 by The Rosen Publishing Group, Inc.
29 East 21st Street, New York, NY 10010

First Edition

Library of Congress Cataloging-in-Publication Data

Marx, Christy.
The Wachowski brothers : creators of the Matrix / by Christy Marx.
    p. cm. —(Famous families)
Filmography: p.
Includes bibliographical references and index.
ISBN 1-4042-0264-1 (library binding)
1. Wachowski, Larry, 1965– 2. Wachowski, Andy, 1967– 3. Motion picture producers and directors—United States—Biography.
I. Title. II. Series.
PN1998.3.W33M37 2004
791.4302'33'092273—dc22

                                                                    2004012880

Manufactured in the United States of America

Contents

THE POWER OF TWO

On March 31, 1999, an unknown movie by a pair of unknown filmmakers exploded on movie screens with a phenomenal impact. *The Matrix* was a major hit, raking in $171 million in the United States and another $270 million overseas. *The Matrix* was part of a trilogy that made around $600 million in the United States alone. And that's not counting the sales of DVDs, VHS tapes, computer games, and merchandising.

Beyond making money, *The Matrix* trilogy had an impact in the way it combined many forms of popular culture, such as comics, animation, and cyberpunk science fiction, with elements from mythology and philosophy. The movies also set new standards in the field of visual effects.

Two brothers, Larry and Andy Wachowski, were the creative force behind *The Matrix* phenomenon. They seemed to come from out of nowhere to make some of the most profitable and influential science fiction movies of our time.

This image of *The Matrix* (1999) shows a scene from the first chapter of the Wachowski brothers' *Matrix* films. To create scenes like this, the design team built 3D computer models so that every scene in the city and on the hovercraft fleet could be viewed from any angle.

Andy *(far left)* and Larry Wachowski *(center, facing)* always direct their movies together. Although as kids they often argued, which sometimes even lead to fistfights, now they get along very well. Their collaboration has brought them huge commercial and critical success.

While it isn't unusual for a team to work together as writers, it is rare to have a director team. Directing is considered a one-person job. The Directors Guild of America doesn't allow more than one person to take credit as a director, unless a team can show beyond question that they are a genuine team. So far, the most successful director teams have been brothers, such as Peter and Bobby Farrelly *(Dumb and Dumber, There's Something About Mary)*, Joel and Ethan Coen *(Fargo, Raising Arizona, Intolerable Cruelty)*, and Albert and Allen

Hughes *(From Hell, Menace II Society)*. But such director teams are still extremely rare.

There must be something special in the relationship between two brothers who write, direct, and produce major movies together. Unfortunately, it's hard to learn about the Wachowski brothers. A few early interviews exist, but since the release of *The Matrix*, the two brothers have kept their personal lives hidden. In fact, they have it written into their contract with Warner Brothers Studio that they don't have to do interviews—and they don't. They say they want their movies to speak for themselves.

How did they get where they are? What were the steps they took along the way? Who helped them? And how did they achieve their success? It began in Chicago, Illinois.

CHAPTER 1

ALIKE YET DIFFERENT

Larry and Andy Wachowski were born and raised in Chicago, Illinois. They are two years apart in age, with Larry born on June 21, 1965, and Andy born on December 29, 1967. Though they're brothers, it's pretty easy to tell them apart. Andy, though younger, is taller and bigger in build, and sports a short, trimmed goatee and sometimes wears glasses. On the other hand, Larry is shorter, with a slighter build, wears glasses, and often wears gold hoop earrings. They both have a fondness for wearing baseball caps backward, though Larry also frequently wears a stocking cap. Both are considered down-home "regular guys" who love basketball and their families.

Bill Pope, the cinematographer for all of the Wachowski brothers' movies, knows the two quite well. He has described Larry as a fierce jihad warrior and Andy as outgoing, funny, and more willing to give and take in the creative process. Andy generally comes across as more quiet. It's usually Larry

Larry *(bottom right)* and Andy Wachowski often rely on the beautiful architecture and urban structure of their hometown, Chicago *(background image)*, as inspiration for many of their movies' settings. The street names in *The Matrix* are names of real streets in Chicago.

who does most of the talking in documentaries or behind-the-scenes footage, but the brothers will often talk in unison.

Funny Guys

Pope also said the two brothers are still children at heart. In a 2003 *Newsweek* interview, Pope said, "They are their own nine-year-old audience." They joke a lot and laugh at one another's jokes. Both brothers have a typical Midwestern sense of humor, delivering their jokes in a low-key, monotonous tone. They make jokes at their own expense, using humor that keeps them from sounding conceited.

When asked in an Internet chat if they were prepared to become legends, their answer was, "Legends of what?" When asked if they considered appearing in a movie themselves, they wrote, "We're too ugly!"

On another occasion, when asked if they considered themselves to be computer nerds, the brothers' comeback was that only the second part was right—they're just nerds!

The Wachowski brothers' sound designer, Dane Davis, thinks they're both hilarious, but that Andy is especially funny. Davis described Andy as a riot and as someone who could be a stand-up comedian.

"Hanging Out Forever Together"

The brothers jokingly say they started collaborating at age four, but admit it's something they say because they don't know how to answer the question of when they started working together. Larry simply says they've just been "hanging out forever together." Cinematographer Bill Pope said they are best friends who genuinely love and respect each other.

Their mother, Lynne Wachowski, worked as a nurse, but had her own creative outlet as a painter. Their father, Ronald, was a businessman. The brothers have two sisters, but never talk about them, and the sisters refuse to talk to the press.

In a 1999 interview with the *New York Times*, the brothers said that they rarely argued while writing or directing and didn't engage in the kinds of fistfights they had while growing up in Chicago. The brothers often make jokes about letting their mom solve their differences or about flying her to the set every day to settle their arguments. On the set, however, no one ever hears them argue.

Early Influences

The brothers have described their mom and dad as big movie fans. Sometimes their parents would take them out for movie-going sprees, seeing up to three movies a day. The brothers mention *Star Wars* as being "good, fun stuff" and one of the first films they went berserk over as kids. They also liked *Blade Runner*, which they consider a masterpiece.

Along with movies, the brothers grew up with a love for comic books and anime. They named their favorite anime films as *Ghost in the Shell*, *The Ninja Scroll*, and *Akira*. The brothers also loved the over-the-top comic-book artwork of Jack Kirby, a famous comic book artist best known for drawing the early Marvel comics such as *The X-Men*, *The Fantastic Four*, *Thor*, and many others.

Akira was one of the first Japanese animated movies, known as anime, to become popular in America. *Akira* and many other anime films feature futuristic settings and intense action scenes. The Wachowski brothers credit anime as having a big influence on their film careers.

Their love of comics continued well beyond childhood. Anime and comics inspired the brothers' imagination and had a major influence on their future work.

From School to Construction

The brothers attended Whitney Young High School, in Chicago, a prominent school for performing arts and sciences. Larry graduated in 1983, and Andy graduated in 1985. The brothers weren't remembered for doing anything special in high school, but they weren't considered loners or outsiders. Those who went to school with them remember the brothers playing Dungeons & Dragons, a popular role-playing game then and now. Classmates also remember the brothers working on Whitney Young's theater and television program. But they didn't work as actors or performers. Instead, Larry and Andy worked behind the scenes on the technical aspects of the productions. This gave them their earliest exposure to the practical side of putting together a production.

During their high school years the brothers read a lot, too. Consuming books and magazines is something they continue to do to this day. Both brothers are voracious readers, with Larry reading a lot of philosophy and Andy favoring science fiction.

Anime

"Anime" (pronounced AH-nih-may) is simply the Japanese word for "animation." Anime has now come to mean a category of animation produced in Japan. It is known for the unique style of art, characters with oversized eyes and small chins, specialized angles and effects, and more-intricate story lines. Unlike in the United States, where most people continue to think of animation as being for kids, in Japan, anime is produced for a wide range of audiences, from kids to adults. Although anime has been around for decades, it began to have a major effect on the American market in the 1990s and now has a large influence on American pop culture.

Fun Fact

A favorite book that the brothers read and reread is Homer's *The Odyssey*, a great adventure tale of the ancient Greeks. Larry has said that he reads it all the time and always gets something out of it.

After high school, Larry went to Bard College, a four-year liberal arts and science school in the Hudson Valley of New York. Andy, upon his graduation, attended Emerson College in Boston, Massachusetts, a college that focuses exclusively on communication and the arts. At Emerson, Andy took an introductory film class and was considered a top student in that class, despite botching a quiz, according to one professor.

But after a couple of years, the brothers dropped out of their colleges. Back home in Chicago, they teamed up in a construction and house-painting business.

Their First Work as Writers

While running their own business, both brothers married. Andy married Alisa Blasingame in 1991, while Larry married a college sweetheart, Thea Bloom, in 1993. One of the many private jokes in *The Matrix* is the use of the numbers 9/18, which is Alisa's birthday.

It was during these years working in construction and painting houses that the brothers broke into writing for comics. They wrote scripts under Larry's name, although both brothers were doing the writing. They worked for Marvel Comics doing mostly horror scripts for Clive Barker's *Book of the Damned*, *Hellraiser*, and a *Nightbreed* spin-off.

Andy and Larry arrive at the Hollywood premiere of *The Matrix* in 1999. In 2002, Larry separated from his wife, Thea *(far right)*, after nine years of marriage. A divorce settlement between the two is still being worked out by their lawyers.

They also wrote the last seven issues of a nine-issue series created by Clive Barker, the famous horror writer, called *Ectokid*. *Ectokid* is the story of Dex, a fourteen-year-old boy who lives and fights in two worlds—the real world and the Ectosphere, which is the world of ghosts and supernatural powers. *Ectokid* was drawn by artist Steve Skroce, who was just getting his start drawing comics. This would mark the beginning of a long and fruitful partnership between Skroce and the Wachowskis.

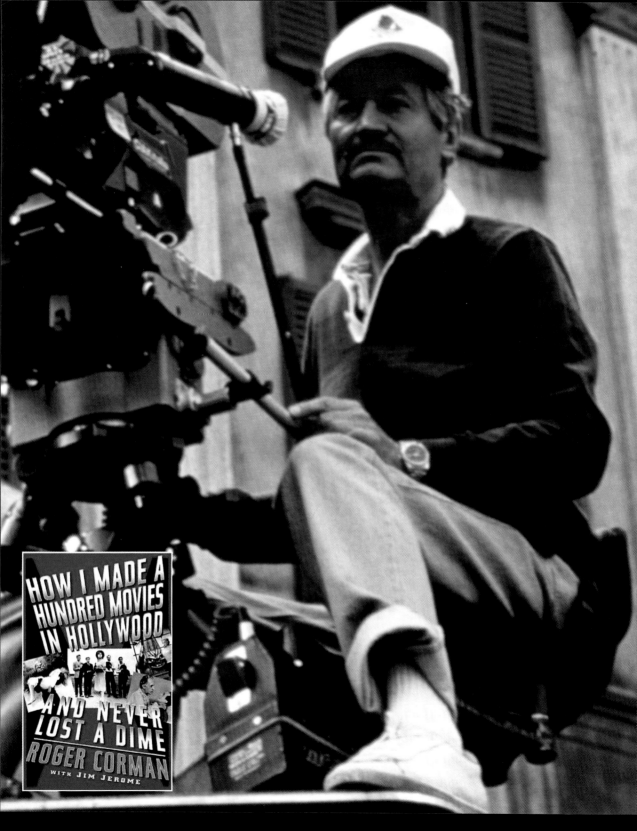

CHAPTER 2

CLIMBING THE LADDER OF SUCCESS

While working in construction and writing for comics, they found a book by independent filmmaker Roger Corman, *How I Made A Hundred Movies in Hollywood and Never Lost a Dime*, covering his busy career making a wide variety of films, such as *Piranha*, *Little Shop of Horrors*, and *The Pit and the Pendulum*. He's also known for giving many famous actors and directors a start in their careers, including Francis Ford Coppola, Martin Scorsese, Jack Nicholson, Sylvester Stallone, and Robert DeNiro.

Carnivore

Inspired by Corman's book, Larry and Andy wrote their first screenplay together. It was titled *Carnivore*, a low-budget horror script about vampirism and rich people being eaten by cannibals. The brothers didn't sell it to Corman, but the script made the rounds in Hollywood. While the dark and disturbing script didn't sell, it did get the brothers some attention.

In this photo from the set of *Frankenstein Unbound* (1990), director Roger Corman, who inspired the Wachowskis to write, keeps a sharp eye on his actors. Inset: The front cover of Corman's book, which is filled with stories on the making of his famously low-budget, or B, movies.

Sylvester Stallone *(left)* and Antonio Banderas play hit men in the Wachowskis' film *Assassins* (1995). The film did not do well with critics or at the box office. Andy and Larry despise *Assassins* and consider it one of the worst films they ever worked on.

Assassins

The first script the brothers sold was for a movie called *Assassins*. The movie was produced and released in 1995 and starred Sylvester Stallone as a hit man who wants to retire. The film also featured Antonio Banderas as a young hit man who is determined to assassinate Stallone. The Wachowskis sold the script to veteran film producer Dino de Laurentiis, who hired big-name director Richard

Donner to direct the film. However, Donner hired another screenwriter to rewrite the script. The Wachowski brothers were so upset by the changes to their script that they tried in vain to take their names off the credits. While the brothers were unsuccessful at distancing themselves from *Assassins*, the experience left them determined not to go through that again.

Early in 1995, they wrote a script based on the popular comic book *Plastic Man*. It turned into another unhappy situation like *Assassins*, in which a director signed on, then rewrote the script. The movie has yet to be made.

Two good things came from those bad experiences. One is that they got to know one of the producers on *Assassins*, Joel Silver. Their relationship with Silver would later allow the Wachowskis to pursue their own projects, in which they would have total creative control.

The other good thing is that *Assassins* made money. This meant that de Laurentiis was extremely happy with the brothers' work and open to other ideas from them. The brothers told de Laurentiis that they wanted to not only write but also direct their next movie. They pitched him the idea for a movie called *Bound*.

Bound

Bound, released in 1996, is about two women, played by Gina Gershon and Jennifer Tilly, who have a lesbian love affair and decide to steal $2 million from a Mafia crime boss. Of course, nothing goes as planned for the two characters. *Bound* was made for a relatively low budget of $6 million. It was moderately successful and became something of a cult hit that got more attention for the brothers. Bill Pope

Andy and Larry monitor the set of *Bound* in 1996. This was the film that convinced Republic Studios that the Wachowskis were talented directors and to give them the go-ahead to make *The Matrix* (1999). The brothers came up with the story of *The Matrix* in 1995 while filming *Assassins*.

was the cinematographer for the film and ended up working on all *The Matrix* movies.

The Wachowskis found that Pope shared with them a love for the visual look of comics, and they drew heavily upon comic books for visual inspiration, especially *Sin City* by writer/artist Frank Miller, who is best known for his work on *Batman: Dark Knight Returns* and the *Elektra* comics.

Proving Themselves

Joel Silver said that he felt the brothers did *Bound* as an audition movie to prove to everyone else, and to themselves, that they knew what they were doing on a movie set. They wanted to play with stereotypes and go against what people were expecting to see. The movie took a standard heist movie concept and added an

unusual twist. The quality of the directing showed that the brothers did, in fact, know what they were doing. It opened the way for the brothers to direct future movies with bigger budgets.

When asked what they say when compared to other brother directing teams, such as the Coen brothers, Larry joked, "We're brothers. They're brothers. We want to be compared to more sisters."

CHAPTER 3

MAKING THE MATRIX A REALITY

As early as high school, the brothers were reading, thinking, and talking about metaphysical subjects such as the nature of reality and perception. While they were writing comics for Marvel and other publishers, a friend asked them if they had any ideas for a new series. They said no, but they started talking about ideas drawn from cyberpunk fiction. Over the course of about three days, the idea that would become *The Matrix* exploded and took form. Pretty soon they had filled notebook after notebook with ideas. The final story line and script came from the ideas jotted in those notebooks.

During the 1990s, Larry and Andy lived near each other on the north side of Chicago. They would write their scripts on large yellow pads, going back and forth to one another's homes to work together. Larry explained that they had a method for crafting their

Andy and Larry on set of *The Matrix* in 1999. At first, many dollies were made in hopes of creating the special effects the old-fashioned way. But the tremendous speed at which the dollies were dragged around the set produced a lot of broken equipment and failed shots, so the brothers decided to use computer graphics instead.

work. They would each work on a part of the script, then switch and rewrite one another's pieces until the script had worked itself out.

Selling The Script

Producer Joel Silver was very supportive of the brothers during the making of *Assassins* and affectionately refers to them as "the boys." One day after a particularly unpleasant experience with the director on *Assassins*, "the boys" mentioned to Silver that they had written something else he might want to read.

Warner Brothers Studio expressed an interest in the Wachowskis, and Silver told the studio that he had the brothers' next script. It was called *The Matrix*. Both Silver and Lorenzo

Joel Silver, the producer of *The Matrix Reloaded*, is shown here at the film's premiere in New York City. His well-known habit of wearing sport shirts and talking loudly and quickly has been parodied in several films.

di Bonaventura, the head of production for Warner Brothers, rallied around the Wachowskis and their script. Silver and di Bonaventura worked for four years to help the Wachowskis' film get made.

The First *Matrix* Comic Book

It was a big jump between a $6 million movie like *Bound* and a giant, special effects spectacular science fiction movie. Most studio executives had trouble fully understanding the complex script. Silver and di Bonaventura suggested that the brothers have the scenes drawn like a comic book to help sell the movie.

Larry and Andy went to artists Steve Skroce and Geof Darrow and began work on a comic book–style storyboard. The brothers were big fans of Darrow, known for his insanely imaginative and unbelievably detailed art style on books such as *Hard Boiled* and *Big Guy and Rusty the Boy Robot*. Darrow became the main design artist for the movie, providing drawings for nearly every aspect of the machine world, such as the sentinels and the machine city, and Zion, the hidden human city. These drawings were then used by the production and art departments to create the models, sets, miniatures, and the computer-generated images.

A storyboard is much like a comic book. It's laid out in panels that match the shape of a movie screen, and it shows, with illustrations, what the shots and camera angles will be. Storyboards are especially used for action and special effects movies to show what movies will look like before they're filmed. The brothers and their artists worked for five months, producing a 600-page, scene-by-scene storyboard that contained every single action beat, visual moment, and stylistic shot in the film. Silver said later that it was virtually identical to the final movie.

Armed with the equivalent of a massive comic book, the brothers were able to go through their script page by page with the studio executives. Their plan worked. The studio executives really got the movie and were excited about it.

Keanu Reeves in *The Matrix*. The time-freezing photographic technique used in the movie was also used by other people in earlier projects, such as a 1998 video clip for pop singer Björk.

Casting a Star

The final piece that had to click into place was signing a big star. The studio brought in Keanu Reeves, who had become a star in the movies *Speed* and *Bill and Ted's Excellent Adventure*. The brothers were a bit hesitant about Reeves at first, until they had a meeting with him. They were immediately impressed by how well Reeves understood the deeper philosophy of the movie. Andy credits Reeves with having total dedication to the role. When they told the actor that this would be the most physically demanding movie ever made, Reeves's eyes lit up with anticipation.

With Keanu Reeves set to star and Joel Silver on board to produce, Warner Brothers gave the project a green light with a $65 million budget. The brothers joked that by this time they had forgiven Silver for *Assassins*.

Where the Ideas Came From

The Wachowskis were out to make an intellectual action movie, what Larry described as "a journey of consciousness." The brothers have said that they like fighting and guns, but were tired of movies that don't have any ideas in them. They wanted to infuse *The Matrix* with as many different kinds of ideas as they could.

Those ideas came from a rich variety of sources. They love *Alice in Wonderland* and put in many references to the book. They were influenced by the books of cyberpunk author William Gibson *(Neuromancer)* and science fiction author Philip K. Dick *(Do Androids Dream of Electric Sheep?*, better known as the movie version, *Blade Runner)*. The brothers were also influenced by J. R. R. Tolkien's *Lord of the Rings* trilogy.

Examining the Nature of Reality

One of the books that had the greatest impact on their ideas for *The Matrix* was by French philosopher Jean Baudrillard. The brothers asked Reeves to read Baudrillard's book before starting the movie to get a deeper understanding of his role for the movie. It's a dense, complex book in which Baudrillard put forth ideas that reality has been replaced by the "hyperreal," which is only an imitation of reality. For example, the Wachowskis point out Las Vegas as a prime example of a place where a hyperreal city has taken the place of reality. There are smaller-scale reconstructions of New York City and Paris, France, created within Las Vegas, so that visitors visit a real place that is still just a fake image of a real place. It blurs the line between what is real and what is fake.

Here is another example of defining what is real: Belgian artist René Magritte created a painting of a pipe. Below the pipe he painted the words, *"Ceci n'est pas une pipe"* (This is not a pipe). He was making a point that while it may look like a pipe, it is only the image of a pipe, not the real thing.

This scene from *The Matrix* shows the virtual reality machinery used to create the matrix. The glyphs on the computer screens are all reversed letters, numbers, and Japanese katakana characters.

These ideas of reality and unreality are the heart of *The Matrix*—that the illusion of reality is so "real" (or "hyperreal") that those inside *The Matrix* (the false reality created by the machines) have no idea that it's not real. And if they can't tell the difference, how can they say for sure what is real and what isn't? These are some of the many concepts the brothers worked into *The Matrix* movies.

The Hong Kong Connection

On the cinematic side, the brothers studied the work of other great directors such as Stanley Kubrick, John Huston, Billy Wilder, Ridley Scott, George Lucas, and Fritz Lang.

They were most strongly influenced by the work of film director John Woo and other Hong Kong filmmakers. The brothers mention Jackie Chan in *Drunken Master II* as a favorite. They feel that American action films simply create fights edited for a flashy impact without engaging the audience members' brains, but the Hong Kong directors actually tell a little story within the fighting.

With that in mind, the Wachowskis hired Yuen Wo Ping, a world-famous Hong Kong director/stunt choreographer, whose mastery of

Significance of Names

Everything in *The Matrix* was carefully thought out by the Wachowskis. The title and all the names in the movie were chosen because they have multiple or deep meanings. The word "matrix" can be mathematical or it can refer to a woman's womb or a mold in which something is shaped. Even the names of characters in *The Matrix* have significant meanings:

- "Nebuchadnezzar" (Morpheus's ship) is from the Bible story in which Nebuchadnezzar, the king of Babylon, has a troubling dream and searches for an answer as to what it means.
- "Neo" (Keanu Reeves) means "new." Neo is also a messiah figure from both biblical and Buddhist mythology.
- "Trinity" (Carrie-Anne Moss) relates to the number three, one of the most sacred numbers in mythology or the holy trinity of the Bible. She is part of the central threesome that also includes Morpheus and Neo.
- "Morpheus" (Laurence Fishburne) is the god of dreams in Greek mythology who can take on any human form he wants.
- "Niobe" (Jada Pinkett Smith) was a mortal woman who compared herself to a goddess in Greek mythology.
- "Persephone" (Monica Bellucci) is a goddess who was kidnapped by the god of the underworld, again from Greek mythology.

wire-harness stunt work can also be seen in *Crouching Tiger, Hidden Dragon*. Using wire harnesses, the actors appear to levitate, fly, whirl, and leap through the sky and across amazing distances. Yuen Wo Ping and his team of talented kung fu stunt actors created all of the martial arts action and stunts for the three *Matrix* movies. Yuen Wo Ping also spent months teaching kung fu moves to the main actors.

The Matrix actors took more than five months to learn the fight moves from martial arts experts. The actors had thought that it would take just a few weeks.

Working as a Team

When it came to the actual directing of *The Matrix* movies, the brothers worked perfectly as a team. Andy said they divided responsibilities pretty much down the middle, about 60 percent for Larry and 40 percent for himself. Bill Pope commented that the good thing about having two directors is that they can act out the movie for you. When you watch the brothers at work in the DVD behind-the-scenes documentaries, you see exactly that. Most often it's Larry looking through the finder (a large, handheld lens device), while Andy performs the action of the shot to show how they want it to look. Or it might be Larry showing an actor how he wants the actor to throw a punch or Andy showing another actor how to react in a scene.

When they weren't acting out the movie, they were sitting in their twin director's chairs, glued to monitors while the scene was being shot. Pope said that when they liked something, they would stick out their lower lips and nod. That was the highest praise you could get from them, and it meant the shot was good. Pope also explained that he had to get both of them—two lower lips and two nods—or he knew they'd have to do the shot all over again.

Silver said it's a mistake to think of the brothers as being one brain in two bodies, but there's no setting aside that they seem to agree on pretty much everything. He watched them a lot and never saw them have a disagreement or argument about anything. Silver concluded the brothers had to have spent a lot of time talking about things ahead of time and had everything worked out by the time they reached the set. Reeves, on the other hand, put it this way about the understanding between the two brothers, "They're one of the most sensitive people I've ever met."

Fun Fact

In one scene in *The Matrix*, Neo passes a television that is showing an episode of the 1960s TV series *The Prisoner*, a show that dealt with a man trapped in "the Village," an artificially constructed reality.

Grueling Work

After *The Matrix* was finally complete, the brothers admitted it was grueling work. In a 1999 interview with the *Orange County Register*, Larry said of completing the film, "I've never been in a war, but it sure felt like that." One of the things that kept them from being overwhelmed by the huge project was their experience in the construction business. Andy explained that in the construction business, they learned to break big jobs down into little steps. By breaking the movie down into little steps, it seemed more manageable and they were able to get through it.

But the wild ride of *The Matrix* was only beginning.

CHAPTER 4

THE MATRIX AND BEYOND

No one knew for sure how *The Matrix* would do, but its meteoric success was beyond what anyone expected. The movie's success was even more surprising considering it was an R-rated film. Beyond the box office, it became the first DVD to sell a million copies.

When the 2000 Academy Awards rolled around, the movie won four awards: Best Editing, Best Sound Effects Editing, Best Visual Effects, and Best Sound. It won or was nominated for many other awards around the world.

Groundbreaking Work

The Matrix included two scenes that became famous for their groundbreaking visual effects. One scene was nicknamed "bullet time"—when Neo bends over backward to avoid bullets as the camera circles around him. The second was "Trinity attack," in which Trinity leaps into the air, remains motionless while the camera circles around her, then completes

Larry and Andy are on *The Matrix* set here in 1999, with actress Carrie-Anne Moss, who plays Trinity in the film. Moss twisted her ankle while shooting one of her scenes. She was afraid of being recast, so she finished shooting the scene injured and did not tell anyone until after the filming.

Keanu Reeves's character, Neo, in *The Matrix*'s famous "bullet time" scene. Although very advanced computer graphics software and lavish sets were the hallmarks of this film, the bullet time sequence relies on a very old-fashioned technique: still photography.

her kick to an enemy. An entirely new process had to be developed to create those effects.

At first, the brothers had an idea that involved putting a camera on a rocket and shooting it around the scene very fast. That proved to be completely impractical. Their visual effects supervisor, John Gaeta, came up with a method that would capture the effect the brothers wanted. Gaeta used a hundred still cameras and a couple of motion cameras set up in a circle surrounding the actor. Each camera was set to shoot images at the same time. These images were then edited together to create the 360-degree circling effect in which time seems to stop.

Soon, other movies came along and copied these effects, including *Charlie's Angels*, *Lara Croft: Tomb Raider*, and *Spider-Man*. Parodies of the Trinity attack showed up all over the place, even in the animated movie *Shrek*. Carrie-Anne Moss, who played Trinity, said that at first the brothers were flattered by the mimicry, then became irritated by it. They were determined to do action scenes and effects in the sequels that took so much time and so much money that they couldn't easily be copied.

The Trilogy

The Matrix dealt with Neo waking up to the real world and joining the human resistance against the domination of the machines. *The Matrix Reloaded* follows Neo's realization that he might not be the savior of the human race as he learns to control his newfound powers and fights the growing threat of Agent Smith. *The Matrix Revolutions* leads to the attack of the machines on the last human city of Zion and Neo's sacrifice to save humanity in a final battle against Agent Smith. In the end, humans and machines agree to a truce.

More Than Just Sequels

There was no question that the sequels to *The Matrix* would be made after the tremendous success of *The Matrix*. The brothers thought of the two sequels as one big movie that had to be cut in the middle. As

In 2003, Carrie-Anne Moss, Laurence Fishburne, and Keanu Reeves teamed up once again in *The Matrix Reloaded*, the second chapter in *The Matrix* film trilogy.

a result, *The Matrix Reloaded* and *The Matrix Revolutions* were shot at the same time with a budget of $300 million. All the principal actors from the original signed on for the sequels without even seeing the scripts.

In 1999, the Wachowskis and Silver went to Japan on a press tour to promote the first movie. While they were in Japan, the brothers wanted to meet some of their favorite anime directors because they were such fans of their work. On the flight home from Japan to Los Angeles, Larry began scribbling diagrams on a yellow notepad on how to have *The Matrix* movies, a video game, and animated stories interact together. They wanted to find high-end Japanese anime directors who would bring their own styles and ideas to the world of *The Matrix*.

Soon *The Animatrix* was born.

The Animatrix

The Animatrix is a special compilation of nine short stories told in various anime styles. The brothers wrote four of the stories and collaborated with the directors on the other five. Their idea was to include material that would set up the second *Matrix* movie.

The brothers wrote "The Final Flight of the Osiris," anime done with realistic computer-generated (CG) graphics. It tells the story of how Zion was warned about the attack of the digging machines. The Osiris is mentioned in the opening scenes of *The Matrix Reloaded.*

Two more Wachowski stories, "The Second Renaissance," part 1 and part 2, are a prequel to *The Matrix*. They tell the story of how humans and machines went to war against one another and how the matrix came to be.

The fourth story the brothers wrote, "Kid's Story," sets up how a boy left the matrix and joined the real world through his belief in Neo. The kid from that story is the one who greets Neo and Trinity in Zion at the beginning of *The Matrix Reloaded*.

Comic Book and Computer Game

In keeping with their love for comics and computer games, the brothers also developed and published *The Matrix Comics*, a collection of comic book stories by various favorite artists and writers. In this collection, the brothers included a story that filled in a piece of the human-machine war history that was mentioned in "The Second Renaissance."

While filming the two sequel movies, the brothers wrote and directed an hour of special footage for the computer game *Enter the Matrix*. The game features Niobe (a ship's pilot from Zion) and fills in another piece of the story that happens between *The Matrix* and *The Matrix Reloaded*.

Setbacks and Tragedies

Making the sequels to *The Matrix* was an epic, exhausting job. The brothers spent a year in preproduction, using Steve Skroce and Geof

Darrow, and once again creating a detailed storyboard for every shot in the films. They spent a year in production of the movies, shooting for seven weeks on a freeway that they had built from scratch on an old U.S. naval base in Alameda, California. After a break of a few months, they went down under, shooting for another 270 days in Sydney, Australia.

Along the way there were setbacks and tragedies. In August 2001, pop star Aaliyah, who had been cast to star in the sequels, was killed in a plane crash. When the original Oracle, Gloria Foster, died of diabetes, she had to be replaced for the third film. And of course, there were the terrorist attacks of September 11, 2001, which deeply affected everyone. In spite of this, production continued later in the fall of 2001.

The brothers didn't forget their family and flew their parents out to visit them for Andy's birthday in December 2001.

Hard Work for the Actors

The movie was also physically tough on the actors, and three of the main actors were injured during the filming. Carrie-Anne Moss broke a leg, Laurence Fishburne fractured an arm, and Hugo Weaving (Agent Smith) put out a disk in his neck doing a wire-harness stunt. Reeves would sometimes sit in a tub filled with ice to ease his aches and pains.

Releasing the Movies

After production of the two sequels, there was another year of post-production in which all the CG and special effects shots had to be completed and all the elements of the movies edited together. *The Matrix Reloaded* was released on May 15, 2003, and *The Matrix Revolutions* was released on November 5, 2003. Both movies made tons of money, firmly establishing the Wachowski brothers' legend as filmmakers. The video game, which cost $20 million out of the film budget to make, made more than $162 million.

Premiere, a major entertainment magazine, annually creates a list of the 100 most powerful people in the entertainment industry. In 2002, the brothers ranked at 89, but in 2003 (the year *The Matrix* sequels were released), they moved up to rank as 27 on the list of 100.

Future Projects

The Wachowski brothers absolutely, positively claim the third movie is the last sequel to *The Matrix*. However, the brothers have continued their make-believe world of *The Matrix* story line with *The Matrix Online*, a MMORPG (massively multi-player on-line role-playing game). The game picks up right where *The Matrix Revolutions* ends and incorporates many of the movies' characters. A skilled player

The Burly Man

In 1991, the Coen brothers made a movie called *Barton Fink*. In their movie, a writer named Barton Fink struggles to write a screenplay about professional wrestling while suffering from writer's block. Soon, bizarre events overtake his once-simple life. The name of his fictitious wrestling screenplay is *The Burly Man*. It would seem that something about this film struck a resounding chord with the Wachowski brothers because "burly" has become one of their favorite words. The fight between Neo and the 100 Agent Smiths is called the "burly brawl." The van the brothers rode in to watch monitors while the freeway scenes were being shot was called the Burly Van. When the Fox studio was handing out passes to visitors, the code name for *Matrix Reloaded* was the Burly Man. And the brothers have named their comic-book publishing company Burlyman Entertainment.

can eventually get to meet and interact with those characters and explore a huge artificial world that re-creates *The Matrix*.

Movie Rumors

Back in 1999, after the success of *The Matrix*, Trimark Pictures acquired the brothers' first script, *Carnivore*. There were press releases that said the brothers would produce and George Romero *(Dawn of the Dead)* would direct, but nothing much has happened since then.

Joel Silver has indicated his willingness to work with the brothers again at any time, but pointed out that after ten years of focusing on *The Matrix* material, the brothers are feeling rather burnt out. He also mentioned, in a November 2003 interview on chud.com, that the brothers wrote a script called *V for Vendetta*, adapted from a graphic novel by famed comics writer Alan Moore. Rumors continue about whether the brothers might produce that film. Other rumors include finally producing their script for *Plastic Man*.

Beyond Movies

Regardless of when they will return to their work behind the movie camera, the Wachowski brothers remain involved in the online game. They have also advertised two other graphic novels to be published by Burlyman Entertainment sometime in 2004: *Doc Frankenstein*, by Steve Skroce and Geof Darrow, and *The Shaolin Cowboy*, by Geof Darrow.

There's really no telling what new universe the Wachowskis will explore next, but one thing seems fairly certain—that they'll explore it together. As Larry said back in 1996, "Well, we're both very, very lazy and having someone else do half the work is very convenient."

TIMELINE

1965	• Laurence Wachowski is born on June 21
1967	• Andrew Wachowski is born on December 29.
1983	• Larry graduates from Whitney Young High School.
1985	• Andy graduates from Whitney Young High School.
1995	• The brothers sell their first screenplay, *Assassins*.
1996	• The brothers write and direct their first movie, *Bound*.
1999	• The brothers release *The Matrix*.
2000– **2003**	• The brothers film and release the two *Matrix* sequels, along with a computer game and graphic novel.
2004	• The brothers work on *The Matrix Online* game.

 **FILMOGRAPHY**

Films and Scripts

1995	• *Carnivore* (not produced)
1995	• *Assassins*
1995	• *Plastic Man* (not produced)
1996	• *Bound*
1999	• *The Matrix*
2001	• *V for Vendetta* (not produced)
	• *The Matrix Revisited*
2003	• *The Animatrix*

        "The Final Flight of the Osiris"
        "The Second Renaissance, Part 1"
        "The Second Renaissance, Part 2"
        "Kid's Story"

• *The Matrix Reloaded*
• *The Matrix Revolutions*

Computer Games

2003	• *Enter the Matrix*
2004	• *The Matrix Online*

Graphic Novel

2003	• *The Matrix Comics*

GLOSSARY

burly Big and strong, of stout build.

cannibal One member of a species eating a member of the same species, such as a human being eating another human being.

cinematographer (or the director of photography) The person responsible for the photography of the motion picture.

cyberpunk A category of science fiction that usually deals with a dark or dangerous future in which the real world and an electronic or digital world have meshed.

Directors Guild of America (DGA) A Hollywood union that represents movie and television directors.

jihad warrior A warrior dedicated to fighting for a principle or a belief.

metaphysical Dealing with the realm of the mind or the supernatural.

R-rated A movie rating that requires anyone under the age of seventeen to be accompanied by a parent or guardian.

stereotype A person or thing that is associated with a standardized mental picture, such as a hard-boiled detective in a trench coat or a square-jawed superhero in tights and a cape.

trilogy A story told in three parts.

American Film Institute
2021 N. Western Avenue
Los Angeles, CA 90027
(323) 856-7600
http://www.afi.com

Warner Brothers Studios
4000 Warner Blvd.
Burbank, CA 91522
(818) 954-3000
http://wbsf.warnerbros.com

Web Sites

Due to the changing nature of Internet links, the Rosen Publishing Group, Inc., has developed an online list of Web sites related to the subject of this book. This site is updated regularly. Please use this link to access the list.

http://www.rosenlinks.com/fafa/wbctm

Corman, Roger. *How I Made a Hundred Movies in Hollywood and Never Lost a Dime.* New York: DaCapo Press, 1998.

Faller, Stephen. *Beyond the Matrix: Revolutions and Revelations.* St. Louis, MO: Chalice Press, 2004.

Haber, Karen. *Exploring the Matrix: Visions of the Cyber Present.* New York: St. Martin's Press, 2003.

Horsley, Jake. *Matrix Warrior: Being the One.* New York: St. Martin's Press, 2003.

Lamm, Spencer, ed., Andy Wachowski, and Larry Wachowski. *The Art of the Matrix.* New York: Newmarket Press, 2001.

Marriott, Michell. *The Matrix Cultural Revolution.* New York: Thunder's Mouth Press, 2003.

BIBLIOGRAPHY

Breznican, Anthony. "Filmmaking Brothers Happy to Hide in the Shadows of Hit '*The Matrix*.' "*Chattanooga (TN) Times Free Press*, May 15, 2003, p. A2.

Gordon, Devin. "*The Matrix* Makers." 2003. Retrieved May 17, 2004 (http://msnbc.msn.com/id/3067730).

Gordon, Devin. "There Were No Easy Shots." 2003. Retrieved May 17, 2004 (http://msnbc.msn.com/id/3069140).

Horowitz, Josh. "The Lost Wachowski Brothers Interview." 1996. Retrieved May 17, 2004 (http://www.moviepoopshoot.com/interviews/27.html).

Koltnow, Barry. "Wachowski Brothers Open Up Just a Hair to Talk About New Film '*The Matrix*'." *The Orange County (CA) Register*, March, 30, 1999.

Matrix Virtual Theatre. Wachowski Brothers Transcript. November 6, 1999. Retrieved May 17, 2004 (http://www.warnervideo.com/matrixevents/wachowski.html).

Miller, Mark. "Matrix Revelations." 2003. Retrieved May 17, 2004 (http://www.wired.com/wired/archive/11.11/matrix.html).

Weinraub, Bernard. "In 'Matrix,' the Wachowski Brothers Unleash a Comic Book of Ideas." 1999. Retrieved May 17, 2004 (http://www.cleave.com/Sight/The_Matrix/wachowski.htm).

Yeffeth, Glenn. *Taking the Red Pill: Science, Philosophy and Religion in The Matrix*. Dallas, TX: BenBella Books, 2003.

INDEX

About the Author

Christy Marx has written for television, film, animation, computer games, and comic books. Among the shows she's written for are *Babylon 5*, *Hypernauts*, *Twilight Zone*, *He-Man*, *Stargate: Infinity*, *X-Men: Evolution*, *Beast Wars*, *ReBoot*, *G.I. Joe*, and *Jem and the Holograms*. Her comics work includes *The Sisterhood of Steel*, *Conan*, *Red Sonja*, and *Elfquest*. Her games work includes *King Arthur*, *Robin Hood*, *Lord of the Rings*, *The Legend of Alon D'ar*, *Tao Feng*, *Earth & Beyond*, and *The Matrix Online*. Christy lives in California with her lifemate and a horde of cats. Visit her Web site at www.christymarx.com.

Photo Credits

Cover © All Star/Globe Photos, Inc.; p. 1 (left) © Reuters/Corbis; p. 1 (right) © Getty Images; pp. 1 (background), 4, 6, 8 (both insets), 12, 16, 18, 20, 22, 24, 26, 28, 30, 32, 34, 36 © Everett Collection, Inc.; p. 8 (background) © Alan Schein Photography/Corbis; p. 15 © Lisa Rose/Globe Photos, Inc.

Designer: Nelson Sá; **Editor:** Charles Hofer; **Photo Researcher:** Nelson Sá